Mahogany Musings

Poems For The People • Volume I

GROUNDED IN GLORY

TERESIA SIMMONS

Mahogany Musings Book Series, Poems for the People Volume I,
Grounded in Glory

Published in the United States, Aiseret Publishing.
Teresia.Simmons@gmail.com

First Edition
ISBN: 979-8-9859966-0-9

Dedication

To my parents Leonard and Lela (Lytle) Hall who never stopped believing in me. You gave us the skills to cope with the uncertainties in life, letting us know that with love in God and family, we could achieve our dreams inspite of the hardships.

You instilled values, spiritual growth, discipline, love, commitment and made many sacrifices in the name of being our parents. Thank you for continuous prayers over your children.

I am blessed to be yours.

Thank you!

Contents

Musings

Broken dreams
Unfulfilled desire
Discarded plans
Lost adventures
Unseen and unknown images
Souls lost
Panic ensued
Ghostly ghastly events
Faith strengthened
Foundations shaken
But not destroyed
The greatest of these is love
Resolve in
God's faithfulness remains

A Divine Diva

A Divine Diva
Is one who belongs to the Lord
She who emotes
Bravery
Confidence
Fortitude
Savor faire
Strength

A Divine Diva
Is bold
In defense of herself
Her man
Her child

A Divine Diva
Is led by the Lord
Who pronounced her worth
She declares the Lord to be Holy and worthy of
Honor

A Divine Diva
Is sure of herself
Sure of her salvation
Confident in her covering
Covered in all her ways

Every day she is covered by the
Blood of Jesus
Covered
Led by the Holy Ghost
Grounded in the word

A Divine Diva
Is brave
Bold and
Unashamed

A New Day

The day has begun
Enough already.
Relax and change.
Ever-evolving changes.
Still Changing.
I must meet me again.
I must create.
Hoping for a new beginning.
Always facing the task of a new me.
Life changes.

A Parent's Plea

Dear God,
It's me crying out yet again.
Help me to guide these young people and show
Them love.
It's so hard.
When I can see the mistakes and
Pitfalls in their way,
Help me to encourage, not hurt.
Help me to guide, not command.
Help me to be an example of Your way,
Your truth and Your light.

Amen

A Reprieve

A Respite
Solitude
Quietness

A reprieve
Time to reflect
Aimless mental thoughts
Random thoughts
Brief spurts of energy

A reprieve
No responsibilities
Joyful phone calls that catch us up
Praying
Thinking
Healing
Warmth
Needs met
Sharing
A respite
A peace

Moments of reprieve

A Rewarder

He is a rewarder of those who diligently seek
Him

Lord, I am seeking your face
I cannot make this journey without you
I am earnestly seeking your face
Oh Lord
My God
I am seeking and praying for your Mercy
Your Grace
Your Help
This poor Soul is seeking Your Face
Praying for Your Mercy
Your Grace
And Your Love

He is our Rewarder

A Special Gift

God gave us a special gift
In the birth and life of our loved one

A special gift of love
Of laughter
Of joy
Of sharing
Of caring
A gift of peace
A gift of music
Beauty
Grace and classiness

God gave us a special gift
A special treasure
A special beauty

The richness of this life
We thank you Lord for the
Special gift of Your child

Lord
We thank You and praise You for
Your goodness and love

And for Your special gift

Adversity

Adversity sharpens the soul
Adversity causes us to tap the source within
Adversity calls upon the reserves of the creative
Stream deep inside our conscious being

Sorrow creates the ability to appreciate what
Once was or to appreciate what now is
Tears of pain teach the preciousness of life

Adversity reminds us of our human frailties
Love reminds us of how
Fragile each person can be

Love teaches the glory of touching another soul
Adversity reminds us of our precarious
Existence in this world

Anger Rails At My Heart

My anger rails at the walls of my heart
I am angry that I let my power,
My self, my joy, be taken away!
I gave my power away!

Yes!
I am angry.
No one has the right or the might
To take away what God gives
To you or to me.
Yet, I did it to myself.
My anger rails at the walls of my heart

Mountains, can you hear my cry?
My howls of hurt?
My shrieks of frustration?
My tears and pain?

My anger is railing, destroying me.
Yes, I allowed this to happen.
I am angry about that too.
But what can I do?
I know.

It will stop with the help of the Lord.
But what can I do?
I can stop.

Realize my mistakes, accept my faults and
Forgive myself.
Forgiving myself means
Reclaiming me and my power.
Letting go of the anger railing at my heart.
My anger for enduring it and
Yes!
God's grace and mercy gives me strength and
Power to control this beast.

Awesome, Lord

Lord, You are so awesome!
Every thing,
Every creature you created has its purpose.

We were created for a purpose.
We were created to worship, adore and be
Happy in You.

Lord, You are awesome!
Mere words or thoughts cannot describe
Your excellence.
We adore You.
We delight in You.

Lord, You are so awesome that we cannot fully
Define, describe or demonstrate
Your Awesomeness!

Behold God Makes All Things New

Behold

He makes all things new
God will do a new thing for you
If you only believe

He allows you a chance to
Clean up
Wash up
And become a new creature for Him

God is
So awesome
So mighty

Behold God makes all things new
Allow Him to wash away
Past hurts
Broken dreams
Old relationships
Old pains
Old obsessions
Broken hearts

Behold God makes all things new
We can stand on His Word

Behold God makes all things new
You can become a new creature
A new believer saved by the grace
And blood of His precious Son
Jesus

Remember
Behold God makes all things new
Arise
Cleansed
Pure
Live your life for Christ
You are a new creature
Saved by grace

Blessed Like That!

Blessed like that!
Lord, we thank You and praise You.

Praise You for our lives
And for Your love.

We know that we are
Blessed like that.

Finally
Securely
Loved and
Blessed like that!

Breathe

Inhale and hold it for a moment
Then exhale
In and out
Filling the very
Core of my heart
With this life force

Relaxing if only for a moment
Concentrating solely on the influx of air

Take in this
Life
Force
That the Supreme Being
God has given to us
This precious gift

The breath of life
We are leaning and surrendering
To the sacred presence of life
Breathe
Just Breathe

Covid 19

A beast raging throughout the world
Blowing it's breath to take away breath from
mankind
Earth is not immune to its path of destruction
Young, old, rich and poor
Irrespective of person, gender or race.

God is showing us His might
A plague sent to remind us of who He is
The beast is raging, destroying and roaming the
Earth.

Yet
We must remember that God is in control
And we must seek His Face
He is able.

The Lord shall heal our land.

Deceptive Practices

Trusting
Needing
Embracing
Only to find
Poisonous pockets of venom, waiting.

Poised to strike
By those we
Trusted, needed and embraced.

Shattered moments of
Trust, broken.

Leery
Distancing ourselves from the destructive
Patterns of People
Places and
Things.

Still
From the burning ashes of destruction
We rise to trust and love
Again.

Envy

Girlfriend!
Who does she think she be?
Who does she think she is?
Humph!
Head all up in the air like she can smell herself?
Just look at her!
She moves about with an attitude!

But girlfriend, I got to give the child some credit
She do be looking good!!!
And,
Her hair is sharp!
Guess I better get my stuff together and
Comb these naps!

And just look at her figure, a cola bottle!
Shoot! She works out every day!
I see her sporting those aerobic tights and
Running shoes.
Pedaling down the street on her bike.
Legs pumping hard.

But girlfriend,
Humph!
She do be looking good!
Maybe I ought to stop worrying 'bout her and
Get my stuff together!

I hates to admit it
But girlfriend,
She do be looking good!
Who does she think she is?

Maybe I ought to get the same attitude.
After all I can do it too.

Does that child think she be the only one that
Can strut her stuff?

Shoot! She better watch out!
'Cause miz thang is gwine to be too fine in just a
Little bit of time!

Humph!
She must think she be something!
But don't tell her I said it!
'Cuz as much as I hates to admit it.
She do be looking good!

Eyes On Jesus

As long as I keep my eyes on Jesus
I can accomplish all my goals.

As long as I keep my eyes on Jesus
Disappointment, sorrow, pain,
Heartache, loneliness, despair
All go away.

As long as I keep my eyes and my heart
Ready to receive His words.
Ready to worship him in spirit and in truth.
As long as I keep my eyes to Jesus
I cannot fail.

He will answer and lead me.
As long as I keep my eyes on Jesus.
My ways, my attitudes and my heart will be
Pleasing to Him.
I am keeping my eyes on Jesus.

God Is Able

In all of my situations,
My thoughts keep returning to God.
He is able!
Through my heartaches,
He is able!
Through my disappointments,
He is able!
Through my sickness and distress,
He is able!
Though I am talked about and ridiculed,
He is able!
Though I lose all that I have,
He is able!
Though my friends turn away and
They are few
In number,
He is able!
Through all of life's crises and situations,
He is able to carry me!
When it is all over and
I am on the other side,
Still -
He is able!
Able to carry.
Able to soothe my lonely heart.
Able to rid me of my addictions.

Able to guide me.
Able to lead me.
Yes!
He is able!
The Lord is able and he sent His Son.
Jesus!
Who left me a
Comforter.
Yes!
God is able!

God's Garden

Pulling, digging, rooting,
Watering, planting, heaping.
Luxuriating in the beauty of this world and all
That God has put into place for me.
He is so awesome.
So magnificent to have created
All this beauty.
Every flower and
Every living thing has a unique pattern.
No two are ever alike.
It is so overwhelming
To try to comprehend the uniqueness of
God and His
Absolute Sovereignty.

Grateful For All The Years

For all the years, the blood, sweat and tears.
For all the struggles, pains, joys and
Moments of happiness.
For the support and the
"Kicks in the butt" when needed.
For the encouragement and the looks that said,
"I didn't birth any quitters, losers, or fools.
You will behave in school."

For the love and the hugs.
For telling us to stay safe and resist drugs.
For never giving up on us and the
Praise the Lord Prayers,
"And the count your blessings praise!"

For telling and showing us
The right way from the wrong.
For never giving up and staying strong.

It would have been easier not to care.
Thank you for just being there.

Some days were probably more
Than you could bear.
Thank God for your belief in knowing that God
Was always here and there!

For the family and siblings and friends.
For the struggles, both financial and emotional.
For the stubbornness, determination and
Stick to it attitude.
For the strong, rooted, belief
In our individual value as persons.
For teaching us the contributions of our people.
Our history and those of our family.

For the encouragement, firmness and love.

We honor you for all the years of trying,
Laughing, crying, working, praying, creating,
Loving, evolving, solving and revolving in your
Journey.

For your faith, courage, wisdom, and
Perseverance.
Thank you! Thank you! Thank you!

Though words can never fully express our love
And gratitude.

We stand here as one.
A living testimony of your love and the seeds of
Your earnest labor.
You shall continually live on because your
legacy remains alive in us all!

We have been blessed!
Wonderfully blessed!
For all the years, we say
Thank you!
We have and are
Standing on the shoulders of giants!
Grateful!

Help!

Lord
You have been my help in the midst of all my
calamities
A steady unwavering friend
My helper
My guide
My way maker
You are my friend

The quiet lonely hours are the times
Of peaceful solitude
Knowing that You are there
That You are here
Lord, You are my help
My shelter in the
Midst of my storms
I am Yours

Homegoing

To everything there is
A season
A time and a place
Each of us has
A purpose, a calling
A reason for being
We have
Seasons of grace
Seasons of peace
Seasons of sorrow
Seasons of despair

Some seasons are those of great joy and
Indescribable beauty
Others are not

The beginnings of life, much like
Spring bring forth the
Promises of great joy and new potentialities
Transitioning into the summer of our lives
We may enjoy lushness, richness, and
Burgeoning promises of easy, lazy days
Luxuriating in the rich, heated passions of love

To everything there is a season and reason
Slowly, we return to the autumn period
As life begins to fade
Change colors, wilt and die
Leaving a beautiful tapestry

As the season changes and life evolves
We become aware of the slowdown
The coolness, the icy tinged fingers brought on
By the frigid air of winter
And the dark, quiet silences in life

To everything there is a season
During and between sunrise and sunset

Our loved one
Came into our lives
Changing from a caterpillar
Morphing into a beautiful creature
And then flying away from us
Constantly changing and evolving
Through all the seasons of their life

To everything
There is a season
A purpose
A reason
We bless the Lord for the granting of these
Seasons of life.

A reason
A time to live
And a time to die
Thank you Lord for these
Seasons
Reasons
Purpose
And for Your Love

Inspired by Ecclesiastics 3:1-2

I Feel So Blessed

God has allowed me to experience this beauty
The breeze glowing
Gently soothing my skin
With gentle kisses and caresses
Soothing me
Calming me
I can feel the awesomeness of
His love and gentle care
I feel so blessed

Thank You Lord
For the loving
For the forgiving
For your guidance
For the ability to
See the beauty
And
Hear sounds of the waves
Lulling me to calmness
And peace
Thankful for it all
I remain grateful
Thank You Lord
I feel so blessed

In His Hands!

Lord
I am remembering when I sometimes forget
I am in Your hands
Through it all

I am in Your hands
Your creation made from dust
Molded by You

I am in Your hands
On my knees praying
Tears streaming down my eyes
I'm in Your hands Lord
Trusting
Depending
Lord
I'm in Your Hands

Issues

What's the problem?
Do you have issues?

Life's given us all
Some unique
Situations.
We all have issues.

Why think yours are more important than
Mine?

We've all had setbacks and heartaches
Failures and mistakes
Issues.

If you can't deal with yours
Leave mine alone!

Issues.

Deal with yours
And
I will deal with mine.

It's So Good

It's so good
To reflect and enjoy the moment
Enjoying the beauty of this day
Thankful for
All the goodness and joy of being alive
It's a good day

I can taste
I can laugh
And
I can smell the beauty all around
Outside and within
I am so thankful for
The greatness and joy of living
It's so good

The Opportunity
To sing
Live and
Be
Enjoying the beauty of each day
It's so good

Lord
Thank You for this day.

Jesus Understands

Jesus understands
All my pain
All my sorrows
He alone can fill my deepest woes
Nobody but Jesus
He knows the feeling of painful words
He knows my deepest despair
Oh thank You Jesus for
Bearing my sorrow
Bearing my pain
Oh Lord
You died for me
Just for me
Just for me

Jesus understands all my pain
All my sorrows
He makes it all bearable
He bore it all for me
Jesus understands my
Pain and my needs
Jesus heals and
Understands

Keep Me, Lord

Please Lord
Keep me in perfect peace
Keep my mind, Lord
Keep my thoughts, Lord
Keep Me
The Word says You
Will keep me in perfect peace
If I keep my mind on Thee
Please Lord, show me
Keep me, Lord
Hold me, Lord
Guide me, Lord
Mold me, Lord
Keep me in Thy will
And in Thy ways
Keep me, please Lord

Life Got in the Way

Just when I thought my goal could be achieved
Life got in the way
This time I was sure it was possible
A sure thing, ready to happen
Then reality set in and once again my plans
Went awry

Once again and then again
I tried to complete my dream
Pursue my passion
Then another delay
Sidetrack
Deviation
Delay
Life threw another curve ball
Still waiting, once again
Delayed dreams
Frustrated
Setbacks

Programmed to put my needs aside
Life got in the way

Lord, Lord

Don't you get tired of me!
I feel so pitiful!
Always complaining,
Whining about this or that!
Hum Drum! Hum!
Never coming to the understanding
That you are always there!
Lord, my omnipresent Lord!
What is man that you are mindful of him?
Thank you Lord,
For you are
Unwavering, unconditional love.
You are awesome and magnificent.
I've felt so pitiful.
Don't get tired of me, Lord!

You're not tired of me?
Your Love fails not!
Your mercies are brand new each and every
Day!
I'm listening, Lord!
I'm feeling Your presence, Lord!

You're faithful!
You'll never leave me alone in my mess!
Thank you Lord for your unwavering,
Unconditional!
Never ending love.
Lord, Lord.

Lord, Guard My Mouth

Lord
I am helpless
A lost child without your
Guiding Spirit

Please guide my path
Lord
Guard my mouth
So my words
Will not inflict pain
Or carry gossip
Lord
Guard my feet
So they will not stray
Lord
Teach me to love like
Jesus
Lord
Guard my mouth

Lord, You Are Our Hope

Lord, you are our hope in times like these.
How do we fathom the hate?
How do we understand what men can do?
What we have done to each other?
What do we tell our children when they see
Such hate in our world?

Our hope is in You.
We are depending on You.
Lord, we place our love, hope and trust in You.
You know what lies ahead.
Lord, please keep us.
Lighten the hearts and souls of all who are lost.
We are depending on you.
We have faith that you will make things better.
In the palm of Your hands.
Lord, we magnify Your name.
Leaning in Your eternal arms.

Lord, You Are My Everything

Lord
You are my hope
You are my joy
And
My Strength
Man fails and has fallen
Yet
You Lord
Center me
Deliver me
Soothe me
Love me
Lord, You are my everything.

My Armor and Shield

Lord, You said we must put on the
Whole armor of
God to withstand the wiles of the devil

Lord
Hold me
Shield me
The fiery darts are winging this way
Help me to hold my peace
To be patient

Shield me Lord
His darts are winging this way

Let me rest beneath Your wings
In the crevice of You, Lord
My rock
My shield
My strong deliverer
My conqueror
My armor
Shield me Lord

New Leaf

I cannot go back
I am capable
Loveable

Worthy of
Respect
Honor
Joy

New miracles each day
A new step
A new joy
A new blessing

I am
Brand new
Fresh
Pure
Refreshing
To God be the Glory

Quiet

Quiet is the void of time
Reflecting upon the inner
Solitude of one's
Soul

Quiet tears not flowing but
Resting deep inside
Ready to
Erupt when
Remembering your love

Quiet
No one to hold
Only memories of what once was

Quiet
Melodies of memories woven into
The fabric of my being

Quiet
Deep
Solitude
Reflections upon what once was

Solitude

Time to reflect
Time to heal
Time to listen to my inner self
Time to hear my own voice

Solitude

What am I about?
What are my needs?
What makes me happy?

Solitude

Listening to my thoughts and prayers
My hopes for the future
My coming to grips with my past

Solitude

Time to forget and
Forgive mistakes of the past
Time to look upon the stars and
Question my role on earth

Solitude

Moments to reflect on God's role
For me in this life

Solitude

Moments spent reflecting on
Important people in my life

Solitude
Thoughts of
Today, the past and my future

Songs Of Praise

Dear God
You have been so good to me
Your wonders to behold
My lips shall eternally sing your praise
Master

Lord
I need your omnipresent Arms
Surrounding me with
Your unconditional compassionate love
Calming and soothing
My soul

Still Standing

Life has a way of wearing one down
It seems circumstances and
Setbacks occur on every bend of the road
Just when one has a glimpse of happiness
Sorrow and pain seem to rear their
Ugly heads and bite

As I crawl out of my valley
Struggling with each step
Beaten back by waves of despair and grief
It seems as though I can't move
Not forward
Nor backward
I am treading water
Until I reach solid ground

Then I remember whose I am and
Who I am in the Lord

I stand up
Weak at first but stronger
I have been strengthened by the blows of life

Then I remember the Lord saying
I will never leave you nor will I forsake you
I will never leave you alone

I am standing
Battered and tattered but standing
Worn from the journey

Still standing on His word
Shedding tears
In pain
But

I am still standing
A survivor
Standing as a witness to His awesome
Strength and power
A witness to His protection
Still Standing

Sunshine Falling On My Face

I am so thankful to the Lord for this day
As I sit
Feeling the warmth of the sun
It feels good just to be alive

There is no need to complain
Because I have been so richly blessed
The warmth and beauty of this day soothes and
Comforts me
Through the rain and the snow
His love for me still shines
He proves His love for me each day
Sending His sunshine and opening up the clouds
To allow the rays to reach me

I am basking in the warmth of His love

The sunshine falling on my face
Is a reminder of his love for me on this day

The Measure

How does one measure their life?
What is the measuring rod?
Is it my standard?
Your standard?
God's standard?
Can one man stand in the judgment of another?
Are you the judge of my life?
Am I the judge of yours?
How do you measure a life well lived?
Did your life make a difference in the life of
Someone else?
Were you all about yourself?
Or about the lives of others?
What is the measure of your life?

The Mysteries Of Motherhood

Why is it that those closest to us
Can hurt us the most?

Why is it that those we have raised and
Sacrificed for
Do us the most harm?

It is a mystery.
A mystery of motherhood.

When we have given so much
Done without so much
Sacrificed so much
Those that are closest to us are able to
Destroy our trust and hurt us the most?

When we have dedicated our
Time, love and attention
Providing
Nurturing
Protecting

How they can reach into our hearts
With heart wrenching
Actions and deeds!

It is a mystery.
A mystery of motherhood.

Lord, please solve this motherhood mystery.
Grant us peace.
Your peace that passes all understanding.
Only You can solve the motherhood mystery.

This Place

This place feels so familiar.
Did I just visit this place?

This same spot at this very same place.
This place of unkempt corners.
Dust motes floating in the same familiar spaces.
The same feelings.
The same endings and beginnings.

Did things really change or will there be no
Difference?
I recognize these same spaces.
These same places.
I've been here before.

Thoughts Of Today

This day is not ours.
It's the Lord's.

What did you do with the life He gave?
Did you share your gift?
Or squander it away?

Did you help someone or hurt them?
Did you give a smile?
Have a kind word?
What did you do to make a difference in the life
Of man?

Did you entertain angels unaware,
Or did you even care?

Life can be short and full of sorrow.

What did you do with the day He gave?

What legacy will you leave this day?

Thoughts On Today And Tomorrow

God is in control
He knows what we are going through
He cares
This season shall also pass
As we bring our attention to
Who He is
His might
His power
His love
His protection
His wisdom
His mercy
His redemption

There shall be no other gods before Him
Money, power, envy, earthly possessions
Shall not stand higher than Him

When we listen and pray
He brings out the best qualities from within His
Children

Forgive us Lord
You are worthy of all glory, honor and praise
Let us never forget
Who You are.

True Friendship

Friends
Care, share, give
Shield and nurture
Friends make the world a little brighter
Joy within the clouds
The love of a good friend
Makes hard landings a little softer
Their embraces encircle our hearts
Friends can
Scold, hold, direct
Correct and love
Friends make the days a little louder and
Smiles a little bigger
Friends leave indelible imprints on
Souls and minds
Friends send prayers and
Special requests of God
Making intercession for you
True friendship is a blessing
Thanks for being a true friend
You are a blessing.

Wedding Commitment

Loved ones
God has blessed you this day to be joined as one
Each of you has traveled different paths
And your circumstances have
Brought you together
This journey of marriage will have many ebbs
And flows through the tides of life
The one constant will be that you are both in
God's hands

It is important for you to remember
That praying and prayers for each other are and
Will be your foundation
Faith is the cement that solidifies bonds
Unconditional love is the
Gold standard of marriage

Look to God who is the author and
Finisher of our faith
God is love
Strive to
Keep God with you in this love
Strive to keep
God first and in the center of your love

Look first to God for His wisdom when
You need direction
Seek happiness and joy
Seek love and kindness
Strive for peace and sharing

Seek common ground and
Learn the compromise and negotiation needed
In a loving relationship

Read Corinthians Chapter 13
And place its principles in your heart
Seek friendship, seek caring
Seek to be yourself
Seek to give of yourself and
Seek to love unconditionally in spite of the
Storms that will come
Storms of illness, financial woes
Misunderstandings
Sorrows and problems of life
Seek the best for each other, love without
Restraint

Two are stronger than one and with
God in the midst and in the middle of your love
There you find a threefold cord
A bond that cannot be broken
Unraveled or strained

On this day, we see two who becoming one
Who will allow each other
To be
To grow
Becoming more in the doing
Together, stronger and better
Constantly, refining each other with the
Sparks of love and sharpening
One another
With your deepening love

Today, you begin this journey
As
Friends, Lovers and
Life partners

These witnesses present at this moment
Wish you love, joy and happiness
We love you

Now
Begin your journey into matrimony and love
Knowing that you are
Blessed beyond measure

We are praying with you and for you in this
journey
We love you

Acknowledgements

I give all honor and glory to my precious Lord for His gift of Jesus and the gifts that He has given to me. I thank Him for His love, guidance and protection.

To Jo Lena Johnson of the Absolute Good Enterprises Publishing Company for seeing the value of my poetry and your earnest and wholehearted support of my writing. Thank you. And the fact that you are my Soror is just so awesome.

To my parents, Lela and Leonard Hall who've always had faith in me. Thanks for your prayers, guidance, spiritual training, sacrifices and your absolute love for me, and for supporting my educational goals and my children. Also, for teaching me to value and love myself, our culture, and our family.

I am grateful for my church families throughout my life: Mt. Zion Missionary Baptist Church in Springfield, Ohio - the late Pastor Rev. W.E. Richardson, Sr., Shiloh Baptist Church in Dayton, Ohio - the late Pastor H. L. Parker. Mt. Zion Baptist Church in East St. Louis, Illinois- the late Pastor John H Rouse. My present church,

Friendly Temple Missionary Baptist Church in St. Louis, Missouri - Bishop Michael F. Jones, Sr. Each of these church families and pastors nurtured my life through their leadership, guidance and biblical teachings.

I am thankful for being a member of Delta Sigma Theta Sorority, Inc., and to my line sisters of the Dayton Alumnae Chapter, La Grande Premiere Fall 1988, who have supported and encouraged me every step of the way. Special love to Beverly Moody and Rachel Johnston. To the St. Louis Alumnae Chapter, special thanks to the Sorors on the June Luncheon Committee who encouraged me to write a poem dedicated to our sisterhood.

To the Redman Writers Guild under the leadership of Dr. Eugene Redmond who welcomed me at all their events with open arms. I especially thank Darlene Roy, also a Delta Soror, who continued to reach out and encourage me. I thank Joyce McKinney for the introduction.

To my St. Louis Sister Friends who have never stopped believing in me: Jeane, Dorothy, Kimberly, Gloria, Georgia, Kwamina, Ruth, NJ, and Mary.

Thanks to Deborah Bennett Peterson who gave me an opportunity to present my poetry at the African Heritage Gala in 1993, at the Dayton

Art Institute for the DCDC Associates. What a memorable experience! This gave me the desire and courage to publish my poetry. Thanks for your unfailing love and support.

To the Ferguson Writers Group with whom I have been a member for well over a decade, our writing retreats and your creative inspiration have been a blessing. And, to Mrs. Carolyn Herkstroeter whose love and encouragement never wavered in wanting to see me as a published poet. Thank you for the opportunity to give a poetry reading to your chapter of the Association of American University Women.

To my Heavenly Angels whose support kept me writing and gave me inspiration because of your love: MaryAnne Mehaffie, Nancy Cox, Craig Wallace, Vinson Taylor and Deanna Mills. Each of you are missed and hold a piece of my heart.

To my lifelong friend Marva Boswell and my cousin Carol Thompson. There's so much to be said for over 60 years! Thanks for being you.

To my 50 year friends, Elaine Stringer and Carolyn Jackson. You are some of the most loving and caring people on this earth. Thank you.

To Marilyn Williams, my friend and fellow member of the Evermoor's. That poetry convention in Washington D.C. was an invaluable experience. Being with you where we were surrounded by published poets, jump started our forty plus year bond as teachers and writers. Thank you!

To Melba, Wyomina, Flora June, Lisa, Lita and Denise, whose love and support are never ending.

To my spiritual "ride or die" sisters whose prayers of love and support have enabled me to continue healing throughout these many years of rough spots. Marva, Yvonnejannai, Lena, Minnie, Crystal, Jacquelyn, Bernice, Carolyn and Pam. And Stephanie, your prayers along with keeping me close when I needed a friend who understood what losing a spouse entailed were lifesaving.

To my siblings Anthony, Christopher and Karen, sister-cousins Monica, Carol and Andrea, thanks for the love we've shared. To my late sister Gloria and Aunt Elverta, I miss you and love you.

To my late husband Joe Simmons who would have been bursting with pride and love to see me performing and signing my books, thank you, my forever and a day love for your support.

About the Author

Author Teresia Simmons grew up in Springfield, Ohio. She is the second child of Lela and Leonard Hall, the second of five children and the first-born daughter. Her parents were married for sixty-four years before her father passed away in 2011. Shortly after, her family mourned the loss of her younger sister, Gloria.

She earned a B.S. in Education from Eastern Kentucky University and a M.S. in Education with special emphasis in Physical education and Dance from the University of Dayton. She became the first African American employee in the Englewood, Ohio, Northmont City Schools, served as a Physical Education teacher.

She married her first husband, Roy Harper in 1971 and from this union, they adopted two children, Randall and Rabiah. The marriage dissolved in after 12 years. She married Joe Simmons in 2000.

She also taught as an adjunct professor at the University of Dayton and Sinclair Community College. She finished her career at Clayton, retiring after thirty years. After marriage, she settled in St. Louis, Missouri, where she became a certified teacher for the Normandy, Jennings and Ferguson Florissant School Systems.

In 2010, Teresia Simmons began working with a small fitness studio, doing individual coaching and teaching in fitness and weight management until her husband Joe was diagnosed with Dementia and needed full time care. He succumbed to the disease in 2019. During that journey, she found great support while volunteering with the Greater Saint Louis Chapter of the Alzheimer's Association, and is now a trained Volunteer Educator. She has also been actively involved with the Friendly Temple (Church) Alzheimer's Support Group, the only African American focused support group in the area.

At present, she is completely retired and loving it. Teresia is an Advisory Board Member and a 17 year member of the St. Louis Symphony Orchestra InUnison Chorus. She also devotes her time volunteering and serving as a member of Friendly Temple Missionary Baptist Church Health Committee, singing in the choir, and helping with the Repast Committee. She is also a member of the Delta Sigma Theta Sorority, Inc., Saint Louis Alumnae Chapter.

Author Teresia Simmons travels and continues to hone her craft by attending writing and poetry workshops, as she finds great joy in creating works of art based on her vast life experiences, including the joy, pain and commitment of love, sickness and health.